TRANSLATED

Translated Language Learning

The Cats of Ulthar
ultar goyangideul
울타르의 고양이들

H.P. Lovecraft

English / hangugeo / 한국어

Copyright © 2023 Tranzlaty
All rights reserved
ISBN: 978-1-83566-239-7
Original text by H.P. Lovecraft
The Cats of Ulthar
Written in 1920 in English
www.tranzlaty.com

The Cats of Ulthar
ultar goyangideul
울타르의 고양이들

Ulthar lies beyond the river Skai
ultarnun sky gang neomeoe issseupnida
울타르는 스카이 강 너머에 있습니다
It is said in Ulthar no man may kill a cat
ultar amudo goyangireul jugil su eopsdago hapnida
울타르에서는 아무도 고양이를 죽일 수 없다고 합니다
and this I can verily believe
geurigo igeoseun naega jinsillo mideul su issseupnida
그리고 이것은 내가 진실로 믿을 수 있습니다
I gaze upon him who sits purring
naneun gyareureunggeorimyeo anja issneun geureul baraboassda
나는 갸르릉거리며 앉아 있는 그를 바라보았다
he lies before the fire
geuneun bull ape nuwo issseupnida
그는 불 앞에 누워 있습니다
because the cat is cryptic
goyangineun bimilser ttaemune
고양이는 비밀스럽기 때문에
and they are close to strange things
geurigo geudeureun isanghan geosdeure gakkapseupnida
그리고 그들은 이상한 것들에 가깝습니다
strange things which men cannot see
sarami boll su eopsneun isanghan geosdeul
사람이 볼 수 없는 이상한 것들
He is the soul of antique Aegyptus
geuneun goldong Aegyptusyoo younghonipnida
그는 골동품 Aegyptus의 영혼입니다
and he is a bearer of tales
geurigo geuneun iyagiui jeondaljaipnida

그리고 그는 이야기의 전달자입니다
tales from forgotten cities in Meroë and Ophir
Meroëwa Ophiryoo ijhyeojin daussy iyagi
Meroë와 Ophir의 잊혀진 도시 이야기
He is the kin of the jungle's lords
geuneun jungle yeong chinjogipnida
그는 정글 영주의 친족입니다
and he is heir to the secrets of hoary
geurigo geuneun Hoaryyoo bimireul gyeseunghapnida
그리고 그는 Hoary의 비밀을 계승합니다
The Sphinx is his cousin
sphink geui sachonipnida
스핑크스는 그의 사촌입니다
and he speaks her language
geurigo geuneun geunyeo eoneoreul gusahapnida
그리고 그는 그녀의 언어를 구사합니다
but he is more ancient than the Sphinx
geureona geuneun sphink de oraedoeossseupnida
그러나 그는 스핑크스보다 더 오래되었습니다
and he remembers that which she hath forgotten
geurigo geuneun geunyeoga ijeobeorin geoseul gieokhapnida
그리고 그는 그녀가 잊어버린 것을 기억합니다

before those in Ulthar forbade the killing of cats
ultar issneun saramdeuri goyangireul jugineun geoseul geumjihagi jeone
울타르에 있는 사람들이 고양이를 죽이는 것을 금지하기 전에
there dwelt an old man and his wife
geogieneun han noungwa geui anaega salgo isseossda
거기에는 한 노인과 그의 아내가 살고 있었다
they delighted in trapping their neighbour's cats

geudeureun yusui goyangireul teocce geollyeoseo
gippeohaesseupnida
그들은 이웃의 고양이를 덫에 걸려서 기뻐했습니다
and they slayed the cats
geurigo geudeureun goyangireul jugyeossseupnida
그리고 그들은 고양이를 죽였습니다
Why they did this I know not
geudeuri wae geuraessneunji naneun moreunda
그들이 왜 그랬는지 나는 모른다
many hate the voice of the cat in the night
manheun saramdeuri bame goyangiui moksorireul silheohapnida
많은 사람들이 밤에 고양이의 목소리를 싫어합니다
and they hate that cats run stealthily in twilight
geurigo geudeureun goyangiga hwanghone mollae dallineun
geoseul silheohapnida
그리고 그들은 고양이가 황혼에 몰래 달리는 것을
싫어합니다
they didn't want cats in their gardens
geudeureun jeongwone goyangiga issneun geoseul wonhaji
anhassseupnida
그들은 정원에 고양이가 있는 것을 원하지 않았습니다
but, whatever the reason:
geureona yuga mueosideun :
그러나 이유가 무엇이든 :
this couple took pleasure in trapping cats
i bubuneun goyangireul japneun geoseul jeulgyeossseupnida
이 부부는 고양이를 잡는 것을 즐겼습니다
every cat that came near their hovel
odumak geuncheoe on modeun goyangi
오두막 근처에 온 모든 고양이
they slayed the cats when they could
geudeureun hal suisseul ttae goyangireul jugyeossseupnida
그들은 할 수있을 때 고양이를 죽였습니다

and they took pleasure in it
geurigo geudeureun geugeoseul gippeohaesseupnida
그리고 그들은 그것을 기뻐했습니다
after dark the villagers heard the sounds
eoduwojija maeul saramdeureun geu sorireul deureossda
어두워지자 마을 사람들은 그 소리를 들었다
the slaying must have been exceedingly peculiar
salhaeneun maewu teugihan geosime teullimeopsda
살해는 매우 특이한 것임에 틀림없다
but the villagers did not discuss such things
geureona maeul saramdeureun geureon ire daehae iyagihaji anhassseupnida
그러나 마을 사람들은 그런 일에 대해 이야기하지 않았습니다
they didn't discuss it much among themselves
geudeureun jagideulkkiri manhi uinonhaji anhassda
그들은 자기들끼리 많이 의논하지 않았다
they didn't discuss it with the old man and his wife either
geudeureun noungwa geui anaewado uinonhaji anhassseupnida
그들은 노인과 그의 아내와도 의논하지 않았습니다
and, because their cottage was so small
geurigo geudeurui odumagi neomu jagass guy ttaemune
그리고 그들의 오두막이 너무 작았 기 때문에
at the back of a neglected yard
bangchidoen madang dwipyeoneseo
방치된 마당 뒤편에서
and it was darkly hidden under spreading oaks
geurigo geugeoseun pyeolchyeojin chamnamu araee eodupge sumgyeojyeoiss
그리고 그것은 펼쳐진 참나무 아래에 어둡게 숨겨져있었습니다
but the truth of the matter was this:
geureona munje jinsireun igeosieossda.
그러나 문제의 진실은 이것이었다.

the cats owners hated these odd folk
goyangi juineun i isanghan saramdeureul silheohaessseupnida
고양이 주인은 이 이상한 사람들을 싫어했습니다

but they feared them more than they hated them
geureona geudeureun geudeureul miwohagibodaneun geudeureul de duryeowohaessda
그러나 그들은 그들을 미워하기보다는 그들을 더 두려워했다

they should have berated them as brutal assassins
geudeureun geudeureul janinhan amsaljaro kkujijeosseoya haesseupnida
그들은 그들을 잔인한 암살자로 꾸짖었어야 했습니다

but instead they kept their cherished pets close
geureona daesin geudeureun seasons awan dongmureul gakkai deudssopnida
그러나 대신 그들은 소중한 애완 동물을 가까이 두었습니다

and they didn't let their loved ones stray
geurigo geudeureun saranghaneun saramdeureul banghwanghaji anhassseupnida
그리고 그들은 사랑하는 사람들을 방황하지 않았습니다

due to unavoidable oversight cats still went missing
eojjeol su eopsneun gamdogeuro inhae goyangineun yeojeonhi siljongdoeossseupneda
어쩔 수 없는 감독으로 인해 고양이는 여전히
실종되었습니다

and sounds would be heard after dark
geurigo eoduwojin hue soriga deullil geosipnida
그리고 어두워진 후에 소리가 들릴 것입니다

the loser would lament impotently
paejaneun muryeokhage hantanhal geosipnida
패자는 무력하게 한탄할 것입니다

or they consoled themselves
ttoneun geudeureun susuroreul wirohaessseupnida
또는 그들은 스스로를 위로했습니다

and they thanked Fate it was not one of their children
geurigo geudeureun unmyeonge gamsahaessseupnida :
geugeoseun geudeurui janyeo jiong hanaga annie eossseupnida
그리고 그들은 운명에 감사했습니다 : 그것은 그들의 자녀 중 하나가 아니었습니다

they tried to be glad it was not a child that vanished
geudeureun sarajin aiga anieossdaneun geoseul gippeoharyeogo noryeokhaessseupnida
그들은 사라진 아이가 아니었다는 것을 기뻐하려고 노력했습니다

because the people of Ulthar were simple
ultar saramdeuri dansunhaessgi ttaemunipnida
울타르 사람들이 단순했기 때문입니다

and they didn't know from where cats came from
geurigo geudeureun goyangiga eodieseo wassneunji mollassseupnida
그리고 그들은 고양이가 어디에서 왔는지 몰랐습니다

One day a caravan of strange wanderers came
eoneu nal naccseon bangrang karaban wassseupnida
어느 날 낯선 방랑자들의 캐러밴이 왔습니다

and they entered the narrow streets of Ulthar
geudeureun ultar jobeun gillo deureogassda
그들은 울타르의 좁은 길로 들어갔다

they were dark wanderers
geudeureun eodumui bangrangjayeossseup
그들은 어둠의 방랑자였습니다

and they were unlike the other roving folk
geurigo geudeureun dareun tteodori saramdeulgwa dallassseupnida
그리고 그들은 다른 떠돌이 사람들과 달랐습니다

the other travellers, who passed through the village
maeureul jinagan dareun yeohaengjadeul
마을을 지나간 다른 여행자들

In the market place they told fortunes for silver
sijangeseo geudeureun eune dahan unserl malhaessseupnida
시장에서 그들은 은에 대한 운세를 말했습니다
and they bought strange beads from the merchants
geurigo geudeureun sangin isanghan guseureul sassseupnida
그리고 그들은 상인들로부터 이상한 구슬을 샀습니다
None knew from what land these wanderers came from
i bangrang eoneu ttangeseo wassneunji amudo mollassseupnida
이 방랑자들이 어느 땅에서 왔는지 아무도 몰랐습니다
but it was seen that they had strange prayers
geureona geudeuri isanghan gidoreul hago issneun geosi boyeossda
그러나 그들이 이상한 기도를 하고 있는 것이 보였다
and they had painted the sides of their wagons
geurigo geudeureun macha cheukmyeoneul chilhaessseupnida
그리고 그들은 마차의 측면을 칠했습니다
strange figures with human bodies
incerl gajin isanghan inmul
인체를 가진 이상한 인물
and the the figures had the heads of cats
geurigo geu inmuldeureun goyangiui meorireul gajigo isseossda
그리고 그 인물들은 고양이의 머리를 가지고 있었다
and hawks, rams, and lions
geurigo mei, sushang, saja
그리고 매, 숫양, 사자
And the leader of the caravan wore a head-dress
geurigo caraban jidojaneun murray jangsigeul ibeossseupnida
그리고 캐러밴의 지도자는 머리 장식을 입었습니다
her head-dress had two horns
geunyeo murray jangsigeneun du gaeui ppuri isseossseupnida
그녀의 머리 장식에는 두 개의 뿔이 있었습니다
and there was the strangest disc between them
geurigo geudeul saieneun gajang isanghan wonbani isseossda

그리고 그들 사이에는 가장 이상한 원반이 있었다

there was a little boy in one of the caravans
carrobane jiong hanae eorin sonyeoniisseossseup
캐러밴 중 하나에 어린 소년이있었습니다
the dark people called him Menes
eodumui saramdeureun geureul menesrago bulleossseupnida
어둠의 사람들은 그를 메네스라고 불렀습니다
this little boy had no father or mother
i eorin sonyeonegeneun abeojido eomeonido eopseossseupnida
이 어린 소년에게는 아버지도 어머니도 없었습니다
he only had a tiny black kitten
geuneun jageun geomeun saekki goyangi man gajigoisseossseupnida
그는 작은 검은 새끼 고양이 만 가지고있었습니다
and he cherished this little cat above all else
geurigo geuneun i jageun goyangireul mueosboda sojunghi yeogyeossseupnida
그리고 그는 이 작은 고양이를 무엇보다 소중히 여겼습니다
the plague had not been kind to him
yeokbyeongeun geuege chinjeolhaji anhassseupnida
역병은 그에게 친절하지 않았습니다
yet it had left him this small furry thing
geureona geugeoseun geuege i jageun teolboksungireul namgyeossseupnida
그러나 그것은 그에게 이 작은 털복숭이를 남겼습니다
it helped to mitigate his sorrow
geugeoseun geui seulpeumeul deoreojuneun de doumi doeeossseupnida
그것은 그의 슬픔을 덜어주는 데 도움이 되었습니다
the very young can find great relief in a kitten
aju eorin saekki goyangineun saekki goyangieseo keun andogameul chajeul su issseupnida

아주 어린 새끼 고양이는 새끼 고양이에서 큰 안도감을 찾을 수 있습니다

the lively antics of a black kitten provides relief
geomeun saekki goyangiui hwalgichan jangnaneun andogameul jegonghapnida
검은 새끼 고양이의 활기찬 장난은 안도감을 제공합니다

So the boy smiled more often than he wept
grasse sonyeoneun ulgiboda misoreul de jaju jieossseupnida
그래서 소년은 울기보다 미소를 더 자주 지었습니다

when he sat playing with his graceful kitten
geuga uahan saekki koyangiwa nolgo anjasseul ttae
그가 우아한 새끼 고양이와 놀고 앉았을 때

on the steps of an oddly painted wagon
isanghage chilhaejin macha gyedaneseo
이상하게 칠해진 마차의 계단에서

On the third morning of the wanderers' stay in Ulthar
bangrang ultar meomun ji saheuljjae doeneun nal achim
방랑자들이 울타르에 머문 지 사흘째 되는 날 아침

Menes could not find his kitten
menesnen saekki goyangireul chajeul su eopseossda
메네스는 새끼 고양이를 찾을 수 없었다

he sobbed aloud in the market-place
geuneun sijangeseo keun soriro heuneukkyeossda
그는 시장에서 큰 소리로 흐느꼈다

some villagers told him of the old man and his wife
eotteon maeul saramdeureun geuege noungwa geui anaee daehae iyagihaessseupnida
어떤 마을 사람들은 그에게 노인과 그의 아내에 대해 이야기했습니다

and they told him of the sounds they heard that night
geurigo geudeureun geunal bame deureossdeon sorie daehae geuege malhaessseupnida

그리고 그들은 그날 밤에 들었던 소리에 대해 그에게
말했습니다

when he heard these things his sobbing gave place to anger

i mareul deureusija, heuneukkyeo uldeon geosi bunnoro bakkwieossda.

이 말을 들으시자, 흐느껴 울던 것이 분노로 바뀌었다.

then his anger gave way to meditation

geureon daeum geui bunnoneun myeongsangeuro bakkwi eossseupnida

그런 다음 그의 분노는 명상으로 바뀌었습니다

and finally his meditation turned to prayer

geurigo machimnae geui muksangeun gidoro bakkwieossda

그리고 마침내 그의 묵상은 기도로 바뀌었다

He stretched out his arms toward the sun

geuneun taeyangeul hyanghae pareul ppeodeossda

그는 태양을 향해 팔을 뻗었다

and he prayed in a tongue no villager could understand

geurigo geuneun maeul saramdeuri aradeureul su eopsneun bangeoneuro gidohayeossda

그리고 그는 마을 사람들이 알아들을 수 없는 방언으로
기도하였다

although, the villagers did not try very hard to understand

geureona maeul saramdeureun ihaehagi wihae yeolsimhi noryeokhaji anhassseupnida

그러나 마을 사람들은 이해하기 위해 열심히 노력하지
않았습니다

because their attention was mostly taken up by the sky

geudeurui gwansimeun taebubun haneure uihae japhyeossgi ttaemunipnida

그들의 관심은 대부분 하늘에 의해 잡혔기 때문입니다

they saw the odd shapes the clouds were assuming

geudeureun gureumi gajeonghago issneun isanghan moyangeul boassda
그들은 구름이 가정하고 있는 이상한 모양을 보았다
the little boy uttered his petition
eorin sonyeoneun tanwonseoreul naebaeteossseupnida
어린 소년은 탄원서를 내뱉었습니다
figures seemed to form overhead; shadowy, nebulous, exotic
suchiga murray wiro hyeongseong geoscheoreom boyeossseupnida. geurimja, mohawm, igukjek
수치가 머리 위로 형성되는 것처럼 보였습니다. 그림자, 모호함, 이국적
hybrid creatures crowned with horn-flanked discs
ppul cheukmyeon discro wanggwaneul sseun hybrid saengmul
뿔 측면 디스크로 왕관을 쓴 하이브리드 생물
Nature is full of such illusions
jayeoneun gruhan hwansangeuro gadeuk cha issseupnida
자연은 그러한 환상으로 가득 차 있습니다
illusions that impress the imaginative
sangsangnyeogeul jageukhaneun hwansang
상상력을 자극하는 환상

That night the wanderers left Ulthar
geunal bam bangrang ultareureul tteonassda
그날 밤 방랑자들은 울타르를 떠났다
and they were never seen again
geurigo geudeureun dasineun boll su eopseossseupnida
그리고 그들은 다시는 볼 수 없었습니다
the villagers were concerned
maeul saramdeureun geokjeonghaessseup
마을 사람들은 걱정했습니다
in all the village there was not a cat to be found
on maeureseo goyangireul chajeul su eopseossseupnida

온 마을에서 고양이를 찾을 수 없었습니다
the cat of each house had vanished
jipjipmada goyangiga sarajyeo isseossda
집집마다 고양이가 사라져 있었다
large and small cats had all vanished
keugo jageun goyangiga modu sarajyeossseupnida
크고 작은 고양이가 모두 사라졌습니다
black, grey, striped, yellow, and white cats
geomeun saek, hoesaek, julmunui, noransaek mukgye huinsaek goyangi
검은 색, 회색, 줄무늬, 노란색 및 흰색 고양이
Old Kranon swore the dark folk had taken the cats away
neulkeun kranone eodumui saramdeuri goyangireul deryeogassdago mangsehate
늙은 크라논은 어둠의 사람들이 고양이를 데려갔다고 맹세했다
in revenge for the killing of Menes' kitten
Menesyoo saekki goyangireul jugin geose dahan boksuro
Menes의 새끼 고양이를 죽인 것에 대한 복수로
he cursed the caravan and the little boy
geuneun carobanceae eorin sonyeoneul jeojuhaessseupnida
그는 캐러밴과 어린 소년을 저주했습니다
But Nith suspected the old man and his wife
geureona Nithneun noungwa geui anaereul uisimhaessseupnida
그러나 Nith는 노인과 그의 아내를 의심했습니다
because their hatred of cats was notorious
koyangie dahan geudeurui jeungoga akmyeong nopassgi ttaemunipnida
고양이에 대한 그들의 증오가 악명 높았기 때문입니다
and they were becoming increasingly bold
geurigo geudeureun jeomjeom de daedam haejigo isseossda
그리고 그들은 점점 더 대담 해지고 있었다
still, no one dared to complain to the sinister couple

geuraedo amudo gamhi saakhan bubuege bulpyeonghaji anhassseupnida
그래도 아무도 감히 사악한 부부에게 불평하지 않았습니다

little Atal vowed that he had seen all the cats of Ulthar
eorin atareun ultar modeun goyangireul boassdago maengsehaesseupnida
어린 아탈은 울타르의 모든 고양이를 보았다고 맹세했습니다
he swore he saw them in that accursed yard
geuneun geu jeojubadeun madangeseo geudeureul boassdago mangsehate
그는 그 저주받은 마당에서 그들을 보았다고 맹세했다
he said he saw them under the trees
geuneun namu araeeseo geudeureul boassdago malhaessda
그는 나무 아래에서 그들을 보았다고 말했다
they were pacing very slowly and solemnly
geudeureun maewu cheoncheonhi geurigo eomsukhage seoseonggeorigo isseossda
그들은 매우 천천히 그리고 엄숙하게 서성거리고 있었다
they moved in a circle around the cottage
geudeureun odumak juwireul woneul geurimyeo umjigyeossseupnida
그들은 오두막 주위를 원을 그리며 움직였습니다
and each cat was next to another
geurigo gak goyangineun dareun goyangi yeopeisseossseupnida
그리고 각 고양이는 다른 고양이 옆에있었습니다
as if in some unheard-of rite of beasts
mazzy jeonrye eopsneun jimseungui uisige issneun geoscheoreom
마치 전례 없는 짐승의 의식에 있는 것처럼
The villagers did not know how much to believe
maeul saramdeureun eolmana mideoya halji mollassseupnida
마을 사람들은 얼마나 믿어야 할지 몰랐습니다
such a small boy may have an imagination

geureon jageun sonyeoneun sangsangnyeogeul gajil su issseupnida
그런 작은 소년은 상상력을 가질 수 있습니다

they did fear the evil pair had bewitched their cats
geudeureun saakhan ssangi goyangireul mahock halkkabwa duryeowohaessdnida
그들은 사악한 쌍이 고양이를 매혹 할까봐 두려워했습니다

they might have bewitched them to their death
geudeureun geudeureul mahoxiceatirn jugyeosseul south issseupnida
그들은 그들을 매혹시켜 죽였을 수도 있습니다

but they preferred not to chide the old man
geureona geudeureun noineul kkujijji anhgireul wonhaessseupnida
그러나 그들은 노인을 꾸짖지 않기를 원했습니다

and so Ulthar went to sleep in vain anger
grasse ultarnun heosdoen bunnoro jamdeureossseupnida
그래서 울타르는 헛된 분노로 잠들었습니다

but the people awaked at dawn
geureona saramdeureun saebyeoge jameseo kkaessda
그러나 사람들은 새벽에 잠에서 깼다

they could not account for what they saw
geudeureun geudeuri bonne geoseul seolmyeong hal su eopseossseupnida
그들은 그들이 본 것을 설명 할 수 없었습니다

every cat was back at his accustomed house!
modeun goyangiga iksukhan jibeuro dorawassseupnida!
모든 고양이가 익숙한 집으로 돌아왔습니다!

Large and small, black, grey
keugo jageun, black, graye
크고 작은, 블랙, 그레이

striped, yellow, and white

julmunui, noransaek mukgye huinsaek
줄무늬, 노란색 및 흰색
every cat had returned
modeun goyangiga dorawassda
모든 고양이가 돌아왔다
the cats appeared sleek and well fed again
goyangineun maekkeureopgo dasi jal meogeun geoscheoreom boyeossseupnida
고양이는 매끄럽고 다시 잘 먹은 것처럼 보였습니다
and they were sonorously purring with content
geurigo geudeureun naeyongeuro gyeongkwaehage gyarrengerigo isseossseupnida
그리고 그들은 내용으로 경쾌하게 갸르릉거리고 있었습니다
The citizens talked with one another of the events
simindeureun sageone daehae seoro iyagihaessseupnida
시민들은 사건에 대해 서로 이야기했습니다
and they marvelled not a little
geurigo geudeureun jogeumdo nollaji anhassda
그리고 그들은 조금도 놀라지 않았다
Old Kranon again insisted that it was the dark folk
neulkeun kranone dasi eodumui saramdeurirago jujanghaessda
늙은 크라논은 다시 어둠의 사람들이라고 주장했다
it was the travellers who had taken them
geudeureul deryeogan geoseun yeohaengjadeurieossda
그들을 데려간 것은 여행자들이었다
because cats did not return from the cottage
goyangiga byeoljangeseo dora oji anhassgi ttaemune
고양이가 별장에서 돌아 오지 않았기 때문에
But all agreed on one thing
geureona modu han gajie donguihaesseubnida
그러나 모두 한 가지에 동의했습니다
the cats would not eat their portions of meat
goyangideureun gogireul meokji anheul geosipnida

고양이들은 고기를 먹지 않을 것입니다
and they didn't drink their saucers of milk
geurigo geudeureun uyu jeopsireul massigi anhassseupnida
그리고 그들은 우유 접시를 마시지 않았습니다
this was exceedingly curious
igeoseun maewu gunggeumhaessseupnida
이것은 매우 궁금했습니다
for two days the cats of Ulthar would touch no food
ettle dongan ultar goyangideureun eumsigeul manjiji anhassda
이틀 동안 울타르의 고양이들은 음식을 만지지 않았다
all they wanted was to doze by the fire or in the sun
geudeuri wonhaessdeon geoseun bull yeopina haesbyeote jolgo issneun geosppunieossseupnida
그들이 원했던 것은 불 옆이나 햇볕에 졸고 있는 것뿐이었습니다

After a week the villagers noticed something
iljuil hu maeul saramdeureun mwongareul ara charyeossda
일주일 후 마을 사람들은 뭔가를 알아 차렸다
no lights turned on in the cottage under the trees
namu arae jeonwonjutaege buri kyeojiji anheum
나무 아래 전원주택에 불이 켜지지 않음
no one had seen the old man or his wife
amudo noinina geui anaereul moshaessseupnida
아무도 노인이나 그의 아내를 못했습니다
not since the night the cats were away
goyangiga tteonan bam ihuroneun anipnida
고양이가 떠난 밤 이후로는 아닙니다
in another week the burgomaster decided to overcome his fears
to dareun jue bureugo maseuteoneun duryeoumeul geukbokhagiro gyeoljeonghaess
또 다른 주에 부르고 마스터는 두려움을 극복하기로 결정했습니다

he called at the strangely silent dwelling
geuneun isanghage joyonghan jibeul bulleossda
그는 이상하게 조용한 집을 불렀다

he was careful to take Shang, the blacksmith
geuneun daejangjangiin shangeul deryeoganeun de josimseureowossda
그는 대장장이인 샹을 데려가는 데 조심스러웠다

and Thul the stone-cutter came too
geurigo doreul jarneun tuldo wassseupnida
그리고 돌을 자르는 툴도 왔습니다

they would be witnesses to what was there
geudeureun geugose issneun geose dahan jeungini doel geosipnida
그들은 그곳에 있는 것에 대한 증인이 될 것입니다

they broke down the old door of the cottage
geudeureun odumagui oraedwen muneul buswo beoryeossseupnida
그들은 오두막의 오래된 문을 부숴 버렸습니다

and this is what they found:
geurigo igeosi geudeuri balgyeon han geosipnida.
그리고 이것이 그들이 발견 한 것입니다.

two cleanly picked human skeletons
kkalkkeumhage gorn inganui hagol du gae
깔끔하게 고른 인간의 해골 두 개

on the earthen floor
heulk badage
흙 바닥에

a number of beetles were crawling in the shadowy corners
manheun ttakjeongbeollega geuneuljin guseogeseo gui danigoisseossseupnida
많은 딱정벌레가 그늘진 구석에서 기어 다니고있었습니다

There was much talk in Ulthar
ultar manheun iyagiga ogassda
울타르에서는 많은 이야기가 오갔다
Zath the coroner disputed with Nith into the evening
geomsigwan Zathneun jeonyeokkkaji Nithwa nonjaengeul beoryeossseupnida
검시관 Zath는 저녁까지 Nith와 논쟁을 벌였습니다
Kranon and Shang and Thul were overwhelmed with questions
Kranongua Shanggua Tuleun jilmune abdodanghaessseupnida
Kranon과 Shang과 Tul은 질문에 압도당했습니다
Even little Atal was closely questioned
eorin ataljochado myeonmilhi simmuneul badassseupnida
어린 아탈조차도 면밀히 심문을 받았습니다
and he was given a sweetmeat as a reward
geurigo geuneun bosangeuro dalkomhan gogireul badassda
그리고 그는 보상으로 달콤한 고기를 받았다
They talked of the old man and his wife
geudeureun noungwa geui anaee daehae iyagihaessseupnida
그들은 노인과 그의 아내에 대해 이야기했습니다
and they talked of the caravan of dark wanderers
geurigo geudeureun eodumui bangrang daesange daehae iyagihaessseupnida
그리고 그들은 어둠의 방랑자들의 대상에 대해 이야기했습니다
they talked of small Menes and his black kitten
geudeureun jageun menes geui geomeun saekki koyangie daehae iyagihaessseupnida
그들은 작은 메네스와 그의 검은 새끼 고양이에 대해 이야기했습니다
they talked of the prayer of Menes
geudeureun menes gidoe daehae iyagihaessseupnida
그들은 메네스의 기도에 대해 이야기했습니다

and they talked of the sky during that prayer
geurigo geudeureun geu guido junge haneure daehae iyagihaessseupnida
그리고 그들은 그 기도 중에 하늘에 대해 이야기했습니다
they talked of the doings of the cats
geudeureun goyangiui haengdonge daehae iyagihaessseupnida
그들은 고양이의 행동에 대해 이야기했습니다
on the night the caravan left
karaban tteonan bame
캐러밴이 떠난 밤에
and they talked of what was later found
geurigo geudeureun najunge balgyeondoen geose daehae iyagihaessseupnida
그리고 그들은 나중에 발견된 것에 대해 이야기했습니다
in the cottage under the dark trees
eoduun namu arae odumageseo
어두운 나무 아래 오두막에서
in the end the burgesses wrote that remarkable law
gyeolguk burgessesneun geu nollaun beopchigeul seossseupnida.
결국 burgesses는 그 놀라운 법칙을 썼습니다.
this law is told of by traders in Hatheg
i beobeun Hathegyoo sangindeure uihae jeonhaejipnida
이 법은 Hatheg의 상인들에 의해 전해집니다
and it is discussed by travellers in Nir
geurigo geugeoseun Niryoo yeohaengjadeure uihae nonuidoepnida
그리고 그것은 Nir의 여행자들에 의해 논의됩니다
in Ulthar, no man may kill a cat
ultar amudo goyangireul jugil su eopsseupnida
울타르에서는 아무도 고양이를 죽일 수 없습니다

www.tranzlaty.com

www.ingramcontent.com/pod-product-compliance
Lightning Source LLC
Chambersburg PA
CBHW012014090526
44590CB00026B/4004